# How to Pray and Receive Financial Miracle

Powerful Prayers for Financial
Miracles, Business and Career
Breakthrough

## KATIE ARMSTRONG

Published By:

**Better Life Media.**

BETTER LIFE WORLD OUTREACH CENTER.

Website: www.BetterLifeWorld.org

Email: info@betterlifeworld.org

This title and others are available for quantity discounts for sale promotions, gifts and evangelism. Visit our website or email us to get started.

Any scripture quotation in this book is taken from the King James Version or New International Version, except where stated. Used by permission.

# CONTENTS.

*"Owe nothing to anyone—except for your obligation to love one another. If you love your neighbor, you will fulfill the requirements of God's law." -*

Romans 13:8

# Fixing My Financial Dryness

Sometime ago, I found myself in a dire financial fix. I needed a financial miracle, and I needed it ASAP. I had to pay some bills or face being insulted by my creditor.

Usually, I had never bothered about praying for money. I believed that God blesses us by the works of our hands. But this time, I found myself where I needed to get some urgent financial assistance.

In our Church, we're taught against borrowing, especially borrowing to support lifestyle. We're told that we can borrow to fund a business idea, but that borrowing to pay rent, support our wardrobe and others does not make sense.

*"Just as the rich rule the poor, so the borrower is servant to the lender."* -

Proverbs 22:7

And I found out that living with that principle has helped me out over the years. But this time, business wasn't doing well and we needed to pay our rent or face being insulted by our landlady.

So I began to pray for financial help. I prayed

several nights and asked God to show us the way out. While doing that I found out in scriptures that we can actually pray for money. Money is part of our needs that God does supply. I also learned there's a way to pray for financial miracle.

God showed me that all the money I would need in my life is here on earth and not in heaven. He is not printing Dollars, Pounds, Euro, naira or Rand in heaven. He showed me how to take control of the matter spiritually and release angels to get the money I want.

Weeks later, after I had started praying for

financial miracle and always declaring things like, "angels of money, go now and bring my money to me. Cause men and women who are connected to my finances to come", I had a call to come and train someone on digital marketing. I went. Unfortunately, the pay was way smaller than I had anticipated. Although, even if the student had paid 5 times the fee I usually charged, it would not have solved my problem.

But while training the student, he came up with some ideas that needed my service. He wanted the jobs executed immediately. At first I was like, "this student could not even pay the normal training fee, how would he get money to pay for something else?"

But while we discussed, he made me an offer that surprised me. And before I could say jack, he paid immediately. No waiting for analysis, reviews, meetings, etc.

The business deal relieved me of the situation; but more importantly, I had learned something. We can pray for a financial miracle when we are in a fix, and there is a way to pray and get answers for financial miracles, career and business breakthrough.

In this book, I will charge you to pray for your finances and get a breakthrough if things seems tough at the moment. Get ready. Something good will happen to you, in Jesus name.

# What Financial Miracle Breakthrough Means.

A miracle is a divine intervention. Something that alters normal course of life and produces a positive effect. For instance, the common way to make money is to render a service or sell a product. Using that definition, one would therefore say that a financial miracle is an intervention that helps someone out of a financial situation without directly rendering a service or selling a product.

While that is accurate, it is however wrong to just peg financial miracle on that premise alone. I believe that financial miracle is encompassing. For instance, if you are working on a job that is not yielding enough money for you at the end of the day, and you seek God about it and pray for several days, and get a raise, or a better offer eventually (say, after a couple of weeks or months) ...that's a financial miracle breakthrough.

If you are in a financial fix and suddenly someone calls you and gives you a job that gives you relief after you have prayed, that's financial breakthrough.

If your business is not doing so well and you spend time seeking God about it, and then eventually get an idea or ideas that transforms everything for you, and gets you back on track to profitability, that's a financial miracle breakthrough.

The Bible says:

---

*"Every good gift and every perfect gift is from above, and cometh down from the Father of lights, with whom is no variableness, neither shadow of turning." – **James 1:17***

---

When praying for financial breakthrough, you should have an open mind. You should not confine God to one specific way to answer your prayers. What matters is that He will answer your prayers, but the manner it would take is entirely at His discretion. Your job is to have faith and maintain an open mind as you pray.

So if you find yourself at a point where you really need a financial assistance, a raise, a push, or you feel that the enemy is threatening your finances, you can pray and loose the angels of goodness and mercy to work and bring your supplies back.

However, there are a few key points I would like to state before we begin to pray and declare the promises of God over our finances.

---

## 1. Financial breakthrough does not mean that money will fall from the sky or that unknown persons will call you and give you huge sums of money for free or that you'll win lotto or football bet.

Someone messaged me the other day and asked me to go watch a video of manna falling from the sky. I said, "for real? Did you watch it?" He said yes and tried to persuade me. Unfortunately, I didn't get to watch the video.

Yes, I know that God can do all things, but it's not a good idea for us to expect manna to fall from the sky. That is, free food. The time we'll spend waiting for manna to fall from the sky and gathering it, we can invest such time in doing creative work and gather more manna from men.

There's also this misunderstanding in our faith churches. One or two persons shares a testimony of how someone called them after prayers and blesses them with money to solve their problems, then everyone claps and praises God. And consequently many believers starts praying and exercising faith that someone will call them and give them money too. Many now believe that if they haven't experienced that kind of miracle, that they've not gotten a financial miracle breakthrough.

That's a wrong mindset. First, I understand that occasionally God can ask people to call us and give us money and gifts. Sometimes such miracles happen to provide relief in serious crisis situations. But as Christians, we are not to live our lives hoping and expecting such occasional interventions as standards for provision.

From my experience, as I shared above, while we pray, God can open doors that is still in line with our businesses and jobs and by rendering services He blesses us with money to take care of our financial situation, and not necessarily raining down cash from heaven or getting someone to give us money for free.

The point is for us not to adore one method of God's provision and insist that's how we're going to be blessed or nothing else.

---

## 2. Financial Miracles can happen from time to time but should not be our only hope to becoming a multi-millionaire without further work.

Most financial miracle breakthroughs are

intended to give relief over present financial crisis situations. But after such miracles, we have to continue to work and or render services and be creative in what we are doing to continue to enjoy financial supplies.

For example, someone shared a story with me some time ago. His friend's wife delivered a baby through a CS. Due to certain complications in the process the hospital bill was a big one. Meanwhile, before this time, this friend was having challenges in his business. So paying the hospital bill and getting his wife out was a big block.

One day, while in the hospital, bowed and in

tears, a man he had never seen before, an Alhaji for that matter, walked up to him and asked what the matter was. In tears, he explained his ordeal. The strange fellow consoled him and paid the hospital bill and gave them some money to go home.

No doubt, that's a financial miracle.

But as you can see, it will be the highest stupidity if this friend refuses to do business or look for a better work and keep hoping that one angel will always bring him money to sort out his problem.

---

*As we pray and seek God in our times of*

*need, we can expect financial miracles from time to time, but it should not be a standard for living.*

---

### 3. Financial breakthrough means a new job with higher pay, a raise in salary, a new business idea or business connection.

The principal way that God blesses His people is through the works of their hands; that is, through your job or career or business. So if you don't have a job and you don't have a business, you can pray for God to give you a job or give you ideas to explore in starting your own business.

Apostle Paul said:

---

*"For even when we were with you, we gave you this rule: "The one who is unwilling to work shall not eat." – I Thessalonians 3:10.*

---

The first thing is to have a willingness to work. Then back up that willingness by making sincere concerted efforts. Then we can pray and command God's blessings over what we are doing.

As we pray, God gives us ideas and shows us

what to do, and connects us with the right people.

---

## 4. Financial breakthrough means divine direction over an investment or career or business decision.

In Genesis chapter 26, there was recession in the land. Isaac wanted to leave the country, but God appeared to him and told him to stay put and invest. He obeyed. The Bible then reports that, "Isaac planted crops in that land and the same year reaped a hundredfold, because the Lord blessed him. The man became rich, and his wealth continued to grow until he became very wealthy." (Genesis 26:12-13).

When there is a business opportunity or job opening before us, we don't just rush into it, no matter how spicy it smells. When things get difficult in our present career or business, we don't just run without looking back. As Christians we spend time and seek the LORD for direction on what to do. He may inspire us to go ahead with what we are doing or explore new doors or stay away. That way we'll be sure to get the best out of such jobs and businesses. That is part of what financial breakthrough is.

But also don't expect everything to be easy because you're a Christian or because you spent 30 days fasting and praying or because you're sure God inspired you to take up the job or start the business or stay put in what you are doing and don't leave. Fasting and praying will clear off spiritual barriers and obstacles but you have to do some digging here and there.

Remember Isaac. It's not easy planting crops when rain won't fall. Isaac had to work out a way to water his crops. He didn't hope that God would send rain on his farm because he heard from God to stay in the land or because he was a covenant child. He and his men dug a deep well; they sweated out the pain and took several days to dig in several places until they found water; and used the water to water their crops.

One thing about God's direction is that you're sure that as you work hard, you'll surely discover water to water your crops. You're working with hope and assurance that at the end you'll have reasons to smile.

## 5. Financial breakthrough also means pulling down the strongholds of the enemy over your finances.

Sometimes the devil can attack your finances, like he did to Job. We may experience losses or extreme difficulty irrespective of how hard we work. When that is the case then you need to stand in God's Word and rebuke the devil.

If you're experiencing great financial challenges which are not as a result of laziness, you can stand in God's WORD and break the power of the devil over your finances. You can command the devil to loose his hold on your finances and release the angels of goodness to bring your finances to you.

That's basically what I did for several nights and broke the enemy's hold over my finances.

# How to Pray for Financial Miracle Breakthrough (Using the Prayers in This Book)

## Surrender to God

The first thing to do when faced with any unpleasant situation is always to humble oneself before God. It's possible you may not know why you've been hit with your present financial situation. It could be an outright attack of Satan on your business, career and finance, or a result of some kind of disobedience, or maybe you're going through a process of change. Whatever has caused the present dryness you are faced with, going before God in humility and asking for His direction and help is the first key to breakthrough.

## Break The Hold of the Enemy.

All through the Bible we see that God wants His people to prosper. He doesn't gain anything when we are lacking finance to care for basic needs. In Matthew 7: 9-11, Jesus said:

---

*9 "Which of you, if your son asks for bread, will give him a stone? 10 Or if he asks for a fish, will give him a snake? 11 If you, then, though you are evil, know how to give good gifts to your children, how much more will your Father in heaven give good gifts to those who ask him!*

If we humans are not that bad towards our children in supporting them, how much more our heavenly Father!

Satan is the one who attacks our means of livelihood and tries to create unnecessary distance between us and God's financial benefits for us. So the right prayer is to command the devil to unfasten his grips over our finances. We must speak with authority and use God's Words to speak to the devil to break his hold.

## Declare The Promises of God.

When any aspect of our lives is under attack, we obtain deliverance and victory by declaring God's promises over and over again in that area of life. For instance, by continuously declaring God's word over our finances, we'll break the hold of the enemy and release our breakthrough. God's Word is what gets us freedom in any aspect of our lives.

## Be Spiritually Alert

You also need to be spiritually alert and sensitive. One way that God answers financial miracle breakthrough prayers is by dropping some ideas or supernatural thoughts in your spirit. These may be new ideas on where to go drop your CV, or persons to approach for business discussion, or outright new business ideas, or anything.

When these unplanned thoughts drop in your spirit, don't despise them. Recognize them and consider following their recommendations, for inside these divine thoughts are hidden our breakthroughs.

Remember Peter's experience in Luke 5. He had toiled all night without a single catch of fish. He and his colleagues were frustrated and confused and needed a breakthrough.

Jesus came on board and after using his boat to preach, told him to cast his net again into the water.

At first, Peter tried to explain to Jesus that fishes don't show up when the water is hot and troubled. That it makes no sense trying to catch a fish during the day, from the same water where they couldn't catch a single fish when the waters were quiet and fishes were more ready to show up.

Nevertheless, he decided to prove to Christ that he (Peter) is right in his view by casting his net into the water. The bible says:

*6 When they had done so, they caught such a large number of fish that their nets began to break. 7 So they signaled their partners in the other boat to come and help them, and they came and filled both boats so full that they began to sink.*

---

That's more like saying, "Peter, I know you've failed in this business. But go ahead and try again."

One thing about divine instructions or the ideas that God puts in our hearts through our prayers and fasting is that they contain the answers we seek. That is why it is highly encouraged that you recognize these divine thoughts, write them down and follow them.

## Fast and Pray

Fasting does not bring money, but it does help you to be spiritually alert to receive instruction from God regarding what you're praying about. It will empower you to break the yoke Satan has placed on your finances and cause you to obtain spiritual breakthrough quicker.

I highly recommend that you fast for a few days (3 days or 7 days) and pray the prayers in this book for your financial miracle breakthrough. Tell God to show you specific actions to take and overcome the situation of financial dryness and receive your breakthrough.

## Leverage on 'The Power of the Night'

What happens in the NIGHT TIMES usually determines the results of the day. That is why occult people mainly have their meetings in the night. The Bible says in Psalm 91:5:

*You will not fear the terror of night, nor the arrow that flies by day*

That simply means that terrors are usually executed in the night times. You know why? Because *"Everyone who does evil hates the day, and will not come into the light for fear that their deeds will be exposed* (John 3:30-Paraphrased).

Jesus said in Matthew 13:25:

*"But while men slept, his enemy came and sowed tares among the wheat, and went his way."*

Enemies utilize the night to sow tares in people's lives because they easily get away without notice. But when we decide to watch and pray in the night, we can destroy whatever the enemies have sown and release our hanging blessings.

During these days you have mapped out to

pray your finances and family out with this prayer outline, let your major prayer time be in the midnight, if possible; that is usually any time from 12:00am - 5am. Through that, you'll accomplish great things. But if not possible, you can still use the prayers anytime of the night

# Prayers for Financial Breakthrough.

---

## 1. REFLECTION AND CONFESSION

**Luke 6:38** - Give, and it shall be given unto you; good measure, pressed down, and shaken together, and running over, shall men give into your bosom. For with the same measure that ye mete withal it shall be measured to you again.

---

**Psalm 35:27 (KJV)** - Let them shout for joy, and be glad, that favour my righteous cause: yea, let them say continually, Let the

LORD be magnified, which hath pleasure in the prosperity of his servant.

---

**Deuteronomy 8:18** - *But thou shalt remember the LORD thy God: for [it is] he that giveth thee power to get wealth, that he may establish his covenant which he sware unto thy fathers, as [it is] this day.*

---

**Philippians 4:19** - But my God shall supply all your need according to his riches in glory by Christ Jesus.

---

**3 John 1:2** - Beloved, I wish above all things that thou mayest prosper and be in health, even as thy soul prospereth.

---

**2 Corinthians 9:8** - And God [is] able to make all grace abound toward you; that ye, always having all sufficiency in all [things], may abound to every good work:

---

**Psalms 1:3** - And he shall be like a tree planted by the rivers of water, that bringeth forth his fruit in his season; his leaf also shall not wither; and whatsoever he doeth shall prosper.

---

## 2. PRAYERS 1 – SUBMISSION:

### 1.

*"Heavenly Father, I give You praise because You delight in the prosperity of Your people. I give You praise because YOU supply my needs according to Your riches in Christ Jesus. Receive my praise today in Jesus name."*

---

### 2.

*"My LORD and my God, How often do I*

*think that prosperity, money and success is*

*by my own efforts and decision alone.*

*LORD, I come to YOU this day and confess*

*my ignorance and pride. Forgive me for not*

*giving YOU the ultimate place in my finances*

*in the past. Forgive me and let Your mercy*

*prevail over me this day, in Jesus name.*

---

## 3.

*O LORD, By the Blood of Jesus Christ, I*

*receive forgiveness of sins. I receive*

*forgiveness for any form of greed and*

*financial impropriety in the past.*

*LORD Jesus, let Your Blood speak for me spiritually from this moment, in Jesus name.*

---

## 4.

*"Thank YOU LORD Jesus because in YOU I have forgiveness of sins. In YOU I have grace to appear before the Almighty God to obtain mercy and find grace in time of need. In YOU I have assurance that when I pray, I receive answers.*

*This is the confidence that I have, that as I pray for my finances this day, I have answers to Your Glory, in Jesus name.*

## 3. PRAYERS 2 – GRACE TO OBEY

### 5.

*"Almighty Father, as it is written in Your WORD, in Job 36:11, that if I obey and serve YOU, that I will spend my days in prosperity and my years in plenty.*

*LORD, I come to YOU this day and ask for grace to obey YOUR Word on finances and in every aspect of life, in Jesus name.*

### 6.

*"HOLY SPIRIT, I come to YOU today, I ask You to make me willing and obedient to the WORD of God henceforth according to Isaiah 1:19 so that I may eat the good things of the land.*

*"Holy Spirit, Uproot every seed of greed and disobedience from me this day, in Jesus name.*

---

## 7.

*"Dear LORD, I ask YOU to make me a blessing in this world, that my life will be a light and support to those who are in need, for it is written that when I give, You will*

command men to give back to me.

*Inspire me to give and to give joyfully without regrets from today, in Jesus name.*

---

8.

*"Holy Spirit, please motivate me and help me to honor the LORD with my resources and finances from this day forward, so that my barns will be full and overflowing with harvest... for it is written in Proverbs 3:9-10:*

**Honor the LORD from your wealth And from the first of all your produce; So your barns will be filled**

*with plenty And your vats will*

*overflow with new wine.*

*O LORD, I desire to obey this WORD. So please Holy Spirit, give me the enablement and direction to obey it, in Jesus name."*

---

## 4. PRAYERS 3 – REBUKE THE ENEMY.

### 9.

*"Heavenly Father, I stand in the authority in the name of Jesus Christ right now.*

*I command every demon working against my business, my career and my finances to* collapse, be bound and cast into the abyss, in

Jesus name.

---

10.

"It is written in Matthew 16:19 that

whatsoever I bind here on earth is bound in

heaven and whatsoever I loose here on earth

is loosed in heaven.

I therefore bind every spirit of poverty, lack,

frustration and loss. I cast them into the

abyss from today, in Jesus name.

---

11.

*"O LORD, based on Your Word we have authority here on this earth and according to (Mark 11:23) we can speak to the mountain and it will have to obey us.*

*So devil, I speak to you in the name of Jesus Christ, I command you to take your hands off my finances right now in the Name of Jesus.*

---

### 12.

*"I speak to the mountain of Lack and Want, I command you to be removed and cast into the sea from this day, in the Name of Jesus Christ.*

## 13.

*"I hereby declare all curses against my life null, void, and destroyed from today. I am redeemed from the curse of poverty! I am free from oppression, in the name of Jesus Christ.*

## 14.

*I now loose the abundance of God, and all that rightfully belongs to me now to start locating me, in Jesus name.*

## 15.

*I thank You O LORD that You have a plan for me to overcome this lack and have abundance.*

*I cast all my cares and money worries over on You Lord.*

*I DECLARE THAT I WILL NOT WORRY anymore, neither will I FRET. I have peace and I'm enjoying God's supplies, in Jesus name.*

---

## 16.

*"It is written that angels are ministering*

spirits sent to minster unto the heirs of salvation.

Therefore LORD, I ask that Your angels of goodness, love and success begin to minister to my needs henceforth, in the name of Jesus Christ.

---

17.

"Wherever my finances are, whoever is connected to my financial breakthroughs, O LORD, let your angels begin to reconnect them to me this day.

As I step out to work on my business or

*career, LORD Jesus, men and women will*

*bring me favor, in Jesus' name.*

---

## 5. PRAYERS 4 –THE POWER TO CREATE WEALTH.

17.

*Heavenly Father, it is written that You give us power to create wealth. Therefore, I ask You to give me the power, wisdom and guidance to create wealth in my life. In Jesus name.*

---

## 18.

*"LORD, I ask YOU today for ideas, I ask YOU for inspiration and divine strategies to turn my career around and grow my business into a global brand.*

*Show me secrets hidden from men and help me to unleash YOUR full potential in what I am doing at the moment, in Jesus name.*

---

## 19.

*"O LORD, make me an employer of labor, so that I will be a blessing to others and fulfill the covenant of Abraham which I inherit in Christ Jesus. Direct me to men and materials*

*that YOU have assigned to bring me into my place of financial and business dominion before the world began, in Jesus name.*

---

20.

*"Holy Spirit, You are my teacher. I ask You to teach me how to make profit in my business and career. Teach me to become a shining light in my business and career. Open my eyes to the right job opportunities and profitable business ventures, in Jesus name.*

---

# 6. PRAYERS 5 – COMMAND THE BLSSINGS.

## 21.

*Heavenly Father, I thank YOU for Your Word, in Psalm 1:3, which says that I am like a tree planted by the riverside. Whatever I do prospers.*

*O LORD, I pray, let Your blessing and prosperity fill my house from this day forward, in Jesus name.*

---

## 22.

*"It is written in 1 Corinthians 9: 8 that God is*

able to make all grace abound toward me; that I, always having all sufficiency in all things, may abound to every good work.

"Therefore LORD, I decree that from this day, I have all sufficiency in all things and I lack nothing. I decree that the grace of God is causing me to abound in every good work, in Jesus name.

---

23.

"It is written in Psalm 112:3 that wealth and riches will be in my house, and his righteousness endures forever.

*"So I decree that my house shall be filled with wealth and riches in Jesus name"*

---

## 24.

*"The Lord is my Shepherd. He prepares a table before me in the presence of my enemies. He anoints my head with oil. My cup runs over with blessings!*

*Money comes to me right now. God is opening the windows of heaven for me. He meets my every need according to His riches in glory by Jesus Christ.*

*He is causing men to give unto me good*

measure, pressed down, shaken together and

running over, in Jesus name

---

## 25.

God has given me the power to get wealth.
I'm blessed in the field. I am blessed going in
and going out. I have the favor of God.
Favor, breakthrough, success, money and
every good thing comes to me from this day,
in Jesus name.

---

26.

*Thank You Father, Thank You Jesus. Thank You Holy Spirit. Together we are creating wealth and lifting men out of lack and want.*

*Thank You for answering my prayers. All Glory is to THEE O LORD, forever and ever.*

# Other Books by the Same Publisher.

1. <u>Prayer Retreat:</u> 500 Powerful Prayers & Declarations to Destroy Stubborn Demonic Problems, Dislodge Every Spiritual Wickedness Against Your Life and Release Your Detained Blessings

2. <u>HEALING PRAYERS & CONFESSIONS:</u> Powerful Daily Meditations, Prayers and Declarations for Total Healing and Divine Health.

3. <u>200 Violent Prayers</u> for Deliverance, Healing and Financial Breakthrough.

4. <u>Hearing God's Voice in Painful Moments</u>: 21 Days Bible Meditations and Prayers to Bring Comfort, Strength and Healing When Grieving for the Loss of Someone You Love.

5 . Healing Prayers: 30 Powerful Prophetic Prayers that Brings Healing and Empower You to Walk in Divine Health.

6. Healing WORDS: 55 Powerful Daily Confessions & Declarations to Activate Your Healing & Walk in Divine Health: Strong Decrees That Invoke Healing for You & Your Loved Ones

7. Prayers That Break Curses and Spells and Release Favors and Breakthroughs.

8. 7 Days Fasting With 120 Powerful Night Prayers for Personal Deliverance and Breakthrough.

9. 100 Powerful Prayers for Your Teenagers: Powerful Promises and Prayers to Let God Take Control of Your Teenagers & Get Them to Experience Love & Fulfillment

10. How to Pray for Your Children Everyday: + 75 Powerful Prayers & Prophetic Declarations to Use and Pray for Your Children's Salvation, Future, Health, Education, Career, Relationship, Protection, etc

11. How to Pray for Your Family: + 70 Powerful Prayers and

Prophetic Declarations for Your Family's Salvation, Healing, Victory, Breakthrough & Total Restoration.

12. <u>Daily Prayer Guide:</u> A Practical Guide to Praying and Getting Results – Learn How to Develop a Powerful Personal Prayer Life

13. <u>Make Him Respect You:</u> 31 Relationship Advice for Women to Make their Men Respect Them.

14. <u>How to Cast Out Demons from Your Home, Office and Property:</u> 100 Powerful Prayers to Cleanse Your Home, Office, Land & Property from Demonic Attacks

15. <u>Praying Through the Book of Psalms:</u> Most Powerful Psalms and Powerful Prayers & Declarations for Every Situation: Birthday, Christmas, Business Ideas, Breakthrough, Deliverance, Healing, Comfort, Exams, Decision Making, Grief, and Many More.

16. <u>STUDENTS' PRAYER BOOK:</u> Powerful Motivation & Guide for Students & Anyone Preparing to Write Exams: Plus 10 Days of Powerful Prayers for Wisdom, Favor,

Protection & Success in Studies, Exams & Life.

17. <u>INNER PEACE</u>: Finding Strength in Difficult Times: Daily Reflections & Powerful Prayers to Find Peace, Encouragement, Strength and Direction in Trying Times.

# Contact Us

---

We love testimonies. We love to hear what God is doing around the world as people draw close to Him in prayer. Please share your story with us.

Also, please consider giving this book a review on Amazon and checking out our other titles.

I also invite you to checkout our website at www.BetterLifeWorld.org and consider joining our newsletter, which we send out once in a while with great tips, testimonies and revelations from God's Word for a victorious living.

Feel free to drop us your prayer request. We will join faith with you and God's power will be released in your life and the issue in question.

# About The Author.

Katie Armstrong is a pastor's wife, school teacher and prayer leader. She has a degree in Medical Physiology and a background as a registered child care professional. Over the years, Katie has seen the effect of prayers on children and families. She encourages parents to spend time and pray for their children and homes with the scriptures and believe God for breakthroughs in life.

She is the women leader and prayer coordinator at Better Life World Outreach Center (www.betterlifeworld.org). She speaks on a variety of subjects like prayer, fasting, food, home care, social media and raising Godly children.

Made in the USA
Thornton, CO
04/17/23 11:45:28

4cf44a6f-1474-448c-a9be-fb08ac12b27cR01